Learn to Write Sight Words - Fruits

The Danger Twins Writing Series

ISBN PAPERBACK: 978-1-956547-06-1

Book design by Anne Lusher

Published by Unplanned Books, LLC.

UNPLANNED BOOKS

A a

Practice tracing
the letters and
then write them.

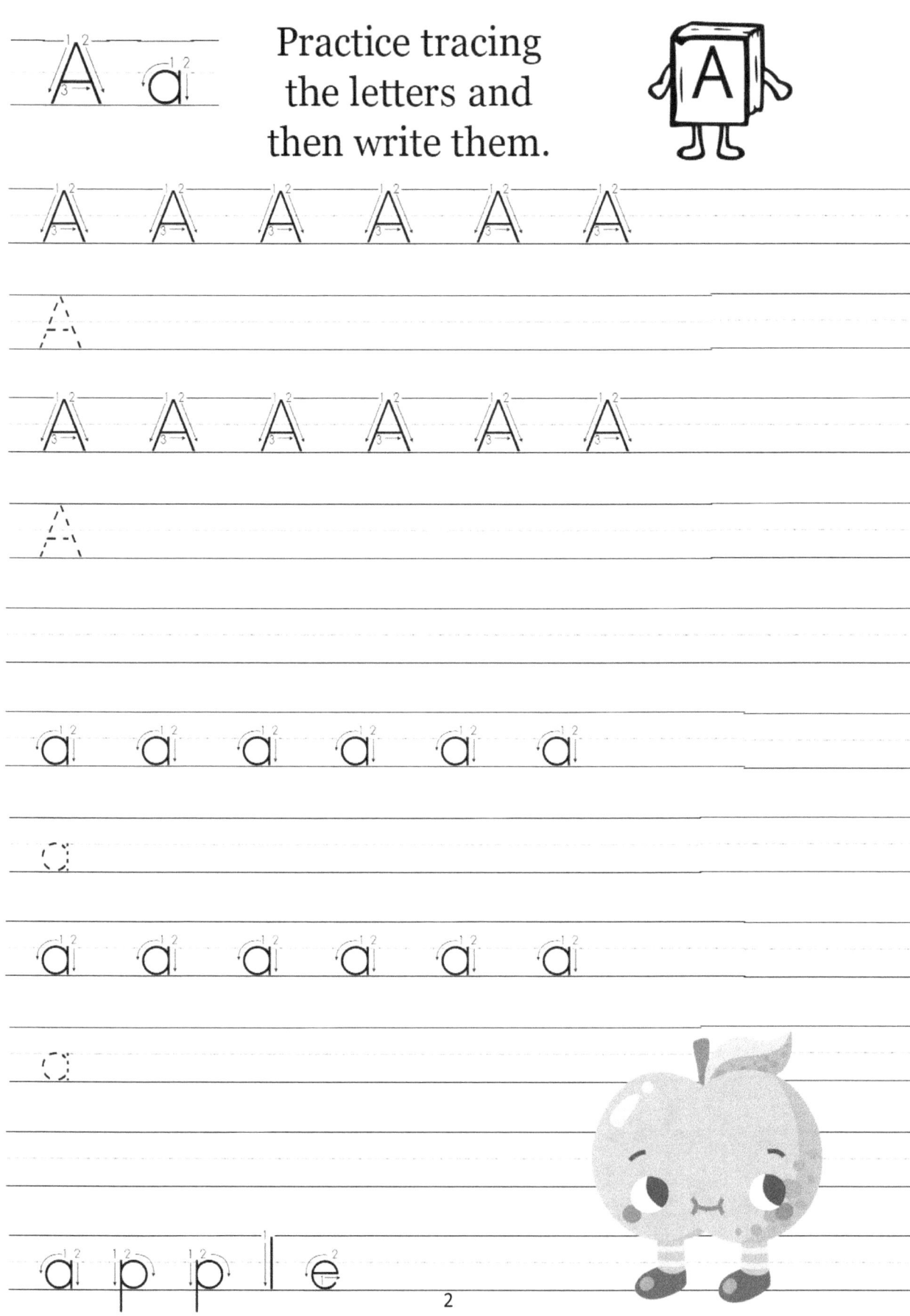

A A A A A A

A

A A A A A A

A

a a a a a a

a

a a a a a a

a

apple

2

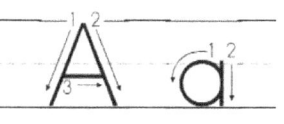 **Practice tracing the sight words and then write them.**

after

after

and

and

ate

ate

apple

apple

A a
Trace and write the sight words, then read aloud the definitions.

A

after

after: later in time

and

and: added to

ate

ate: past tense of eat

apple

apple: a round, edible fruit

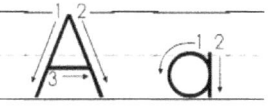 

Use the examples
below to help write
new sentences.

He ate the **apple after** lunch.

I **ate** an apple **and** a banana.

We each **ate** an **apple**.

B b

Practice tracing the letters and then write them.

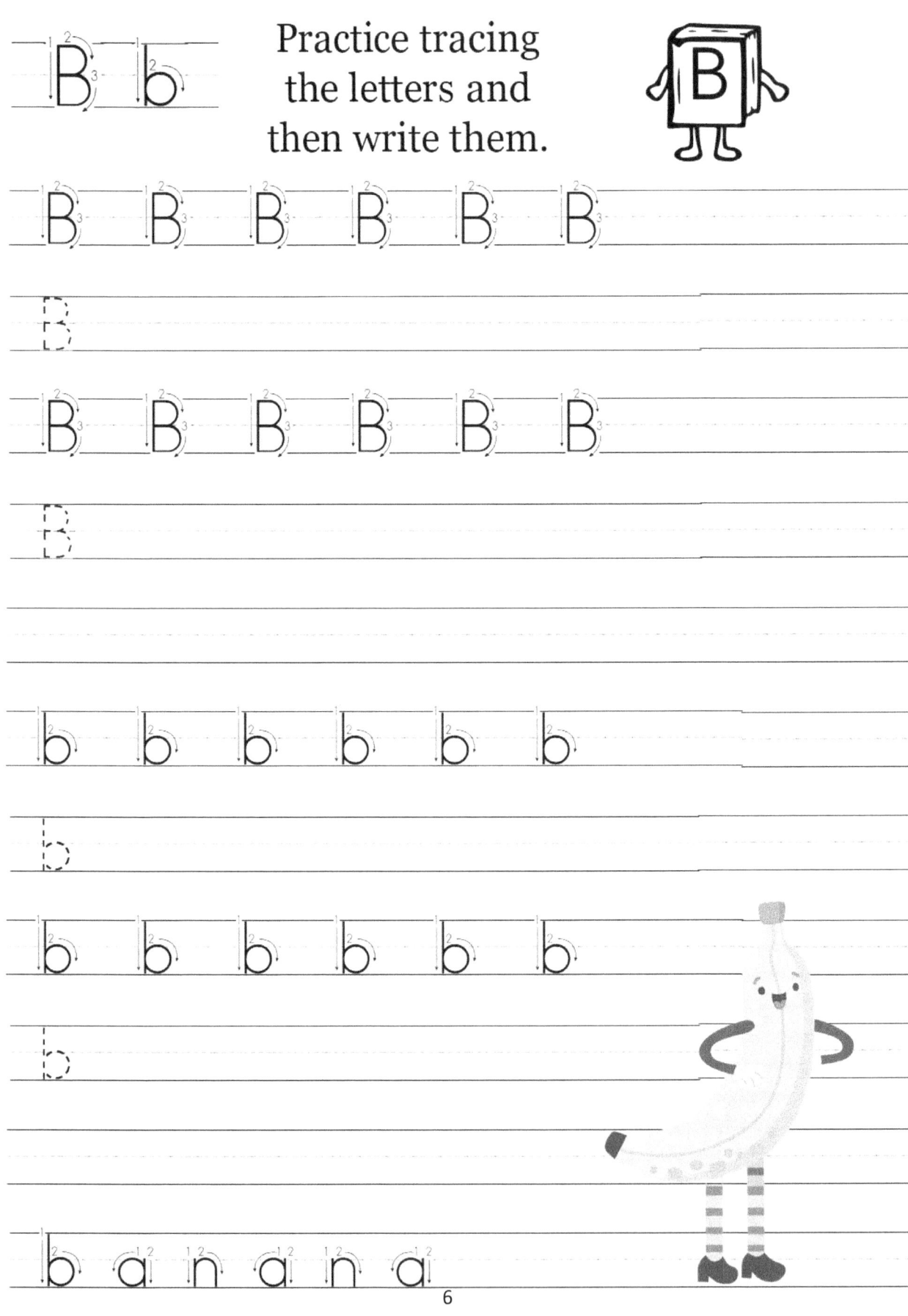

B B B B B B

B

B B B B B B

B

b b b b b b

b

b b b b b b

b

banana

6

Practice tracing the sight words and then write them.

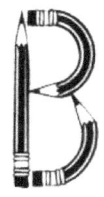

barn

barn

boy

boy

buy

buy

banana

banana

Bb Trace and write the
sight words, then read
aloud the definitions.

B

b a r n

barn: building for storing hay

b o y

boy: a male child

b u y

buy: to purchase

b a n a n a

banana: a tropical plant

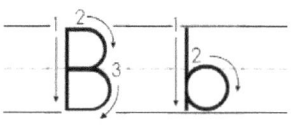 Use the examples
below to help write
new sentences.

The **boy** ran inside the **barn**.

A monkey ate the **banana**.

I want to **buy** an apple.

BONUS WORDS FROM THE DANGER TWINS

The Danger Twins listed additional sight words. Write a sentence using any of the sight words.

all   blue

along   ball

animal   be

C c

Practice tracing the letters and then write them.

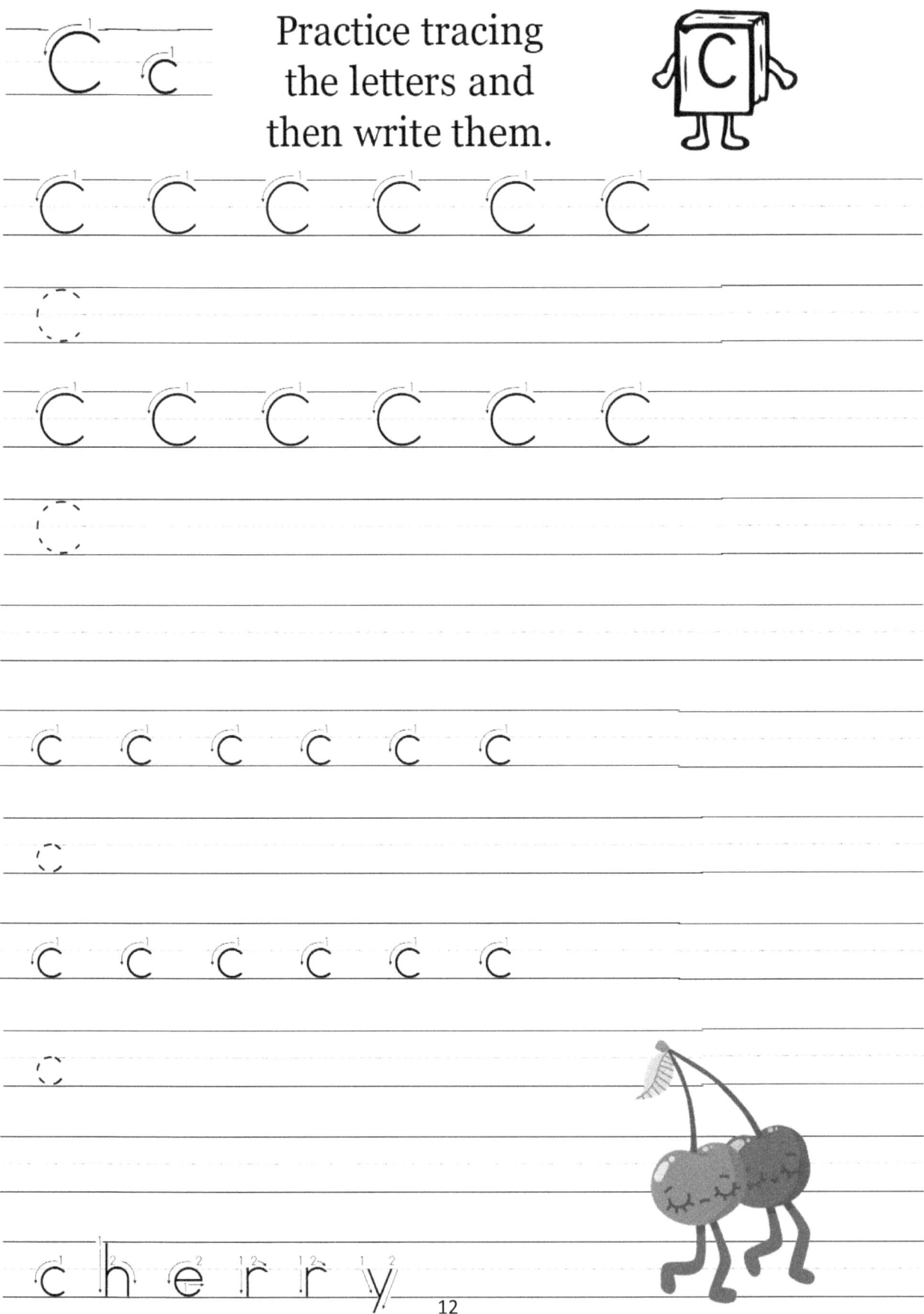

C C C C C C

C

C C C C C

C

c c c c c c

c

c c c c c c

c

cherry

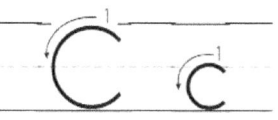

Practice tracing the sight words and then write them.

can

can

carry

carry

child

child

cherry

cherry

C c **Trace and write the sight words, then read aloud the definitions.** C

c a n

can: to be able to

c a r r y

carry: to transport or move

c h i l d

child: a young person

c h e r r y

cherry: a small red fruit

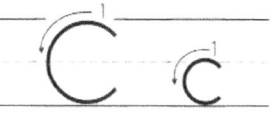 Use the examples
below to help write
new sentences.

She **can** bake a **cherry** pie.

I can **carry** a pound of fruit.

The **child** enjoyed the **cherry**.

D d

Practice tracing the letters and then write them.

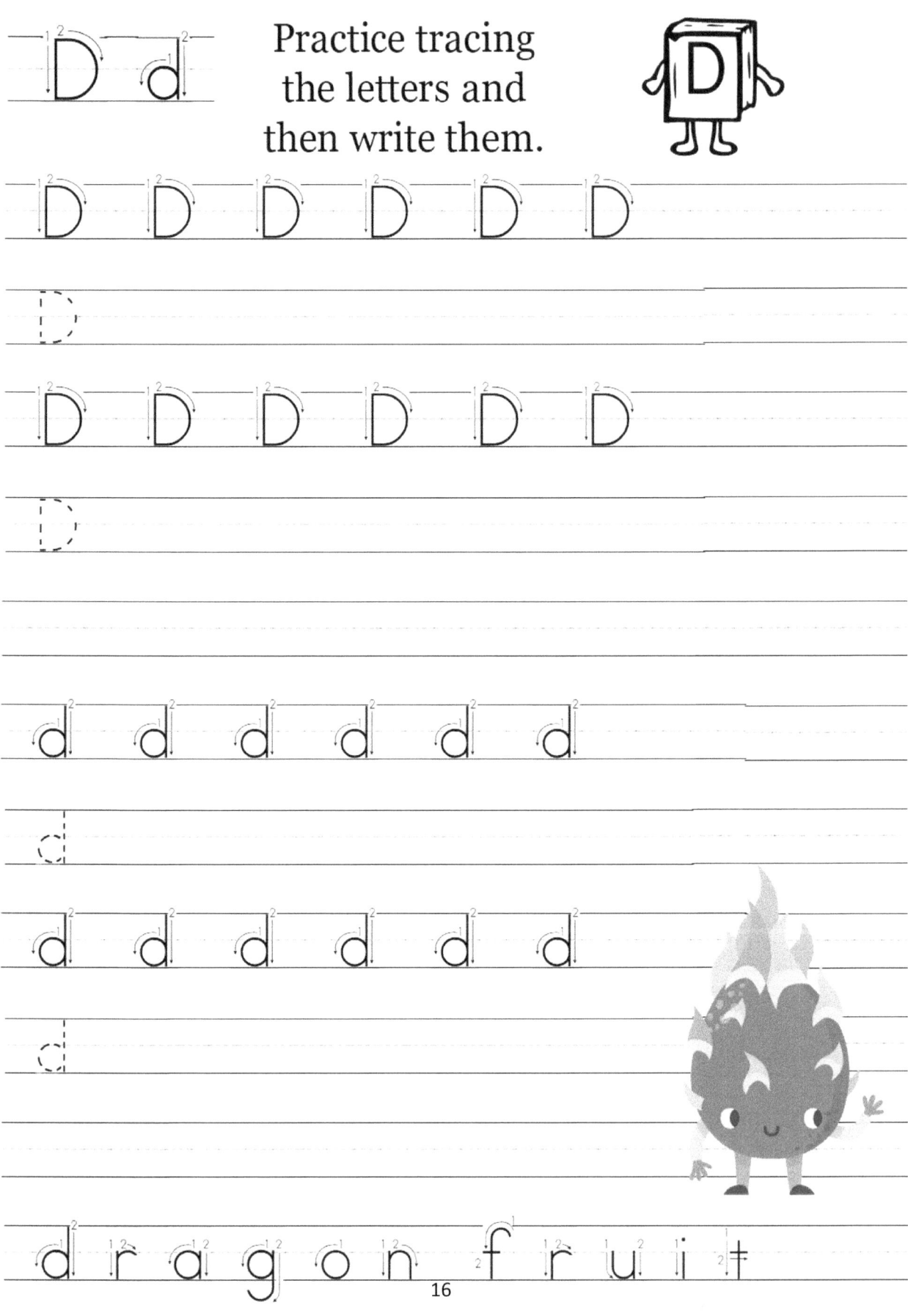

D D D D D D

D

D D D D D D

D

d d d d d d

d

d d d d d d

d

d r a g o n f r u i t

Dd

Practice tracing the sight words and then write them.

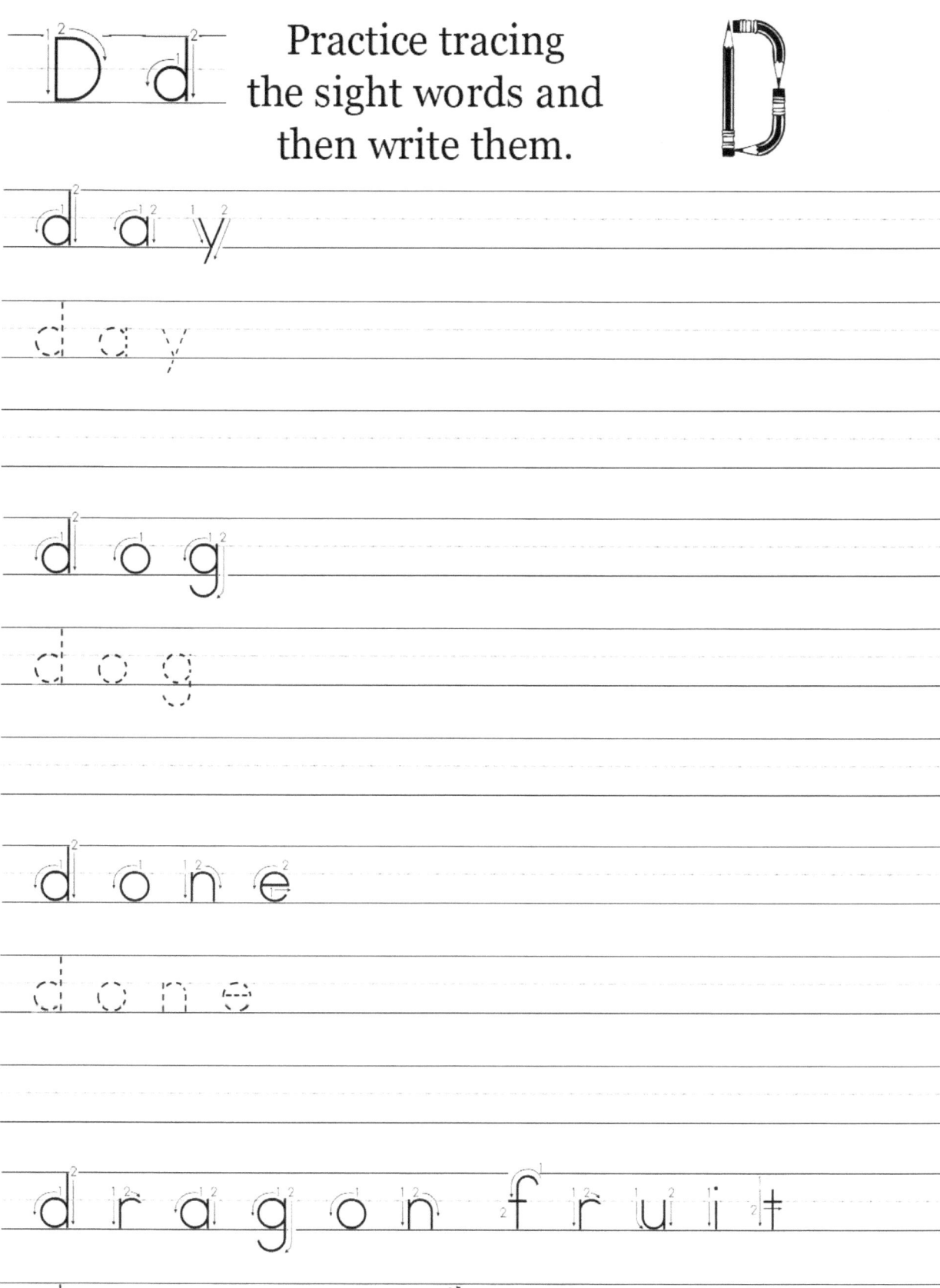

day

day

dog

dog

done

done

dragon fruit

dragon fruit

Dd Trace and write the sight words, then read aloud the definitions. **D**

d a y

day: 24 hours of time

d o g

dog: a domesticated canine

d o n e

done: completed, finished

d r a g o n   f r u i t

dragon fruit: a pointy fruit

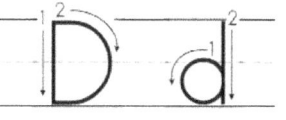 Use the examples
below to help write
new sentences.

The girl eats an apple a **day**.

Our **dog** is **done** eating.

I ate my **dragon fruit**.

BONUS WORDS FROM THE DANGER TWINS

The Danger Twins listed bonus sight words below. Write a sentence using any of the sight words.

circle   drop

cat   drink

chef   dance

E e

Practice tracing the letters and then write them.

E E E E E E

E

E E E E E E

E

e e e e e e

e

e e e e e e

e

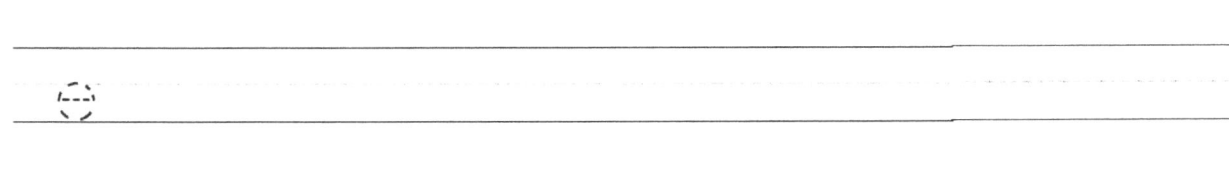

e m u   a p p l e

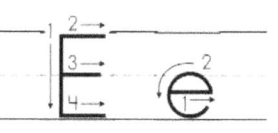

Practice tracing the sight words and then write them.

each

each

enjoy

enjoy

everyone

everyone

emu apple

emu apple

Trace and write the sight words, then read aloud the definitions.

E e

each

each: everyone individually

enjoy

enjoy: take pleasure in

everyone

everyone: every person

emu apple

emu apple: an Australian fruit

24

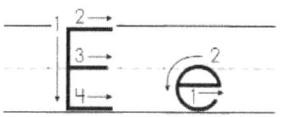 

Use the examples
below to help write
new sentences.

We each ate an emu apple.

I enjoy eating an emu apple.

Everyone likes apples.

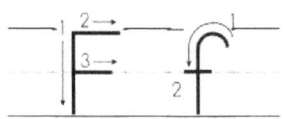

Practice tracing the letters and then write them.

F F F F F F

F

F F F F F F

F

f f f f f f

f

f f f f f f

f

f i g

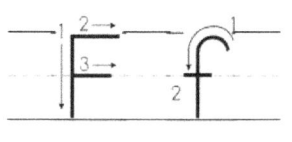

Practice tracing the sight words and then write them.

farm

farm

food

food

fresh

fresh

fig

fig

Ff Trace and write the
sight words, then read
aloud the definitions.

F

farm

farm: land for raising animals

food

food: nourishing substance

fresh

fresh: newly made

fig

fig: a mulberry family fruit

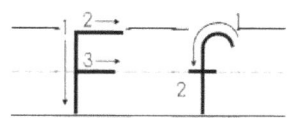 Use the examples
below to help write
new sentences.

The farm has a fig tree.

Fresh food tastes great.

The fruit is fresh.

BONUS WORDS FROM THE DANGER TWINS

The Danger Twins listed bonus sight words below. Write a sentence using any of the sight words.

eat   full

energy   from

entire   find

Practice tracing the letters and then write them.

G g

G G G G G G

G G G G G G

g g g g g g

g g g g g g

guava

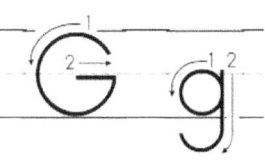 **Practice tracing the sight words and then write them.**

garden

garden

green

green

grow

grow

guava

guava

Trace and write the sight words, then read aloud the definitions.

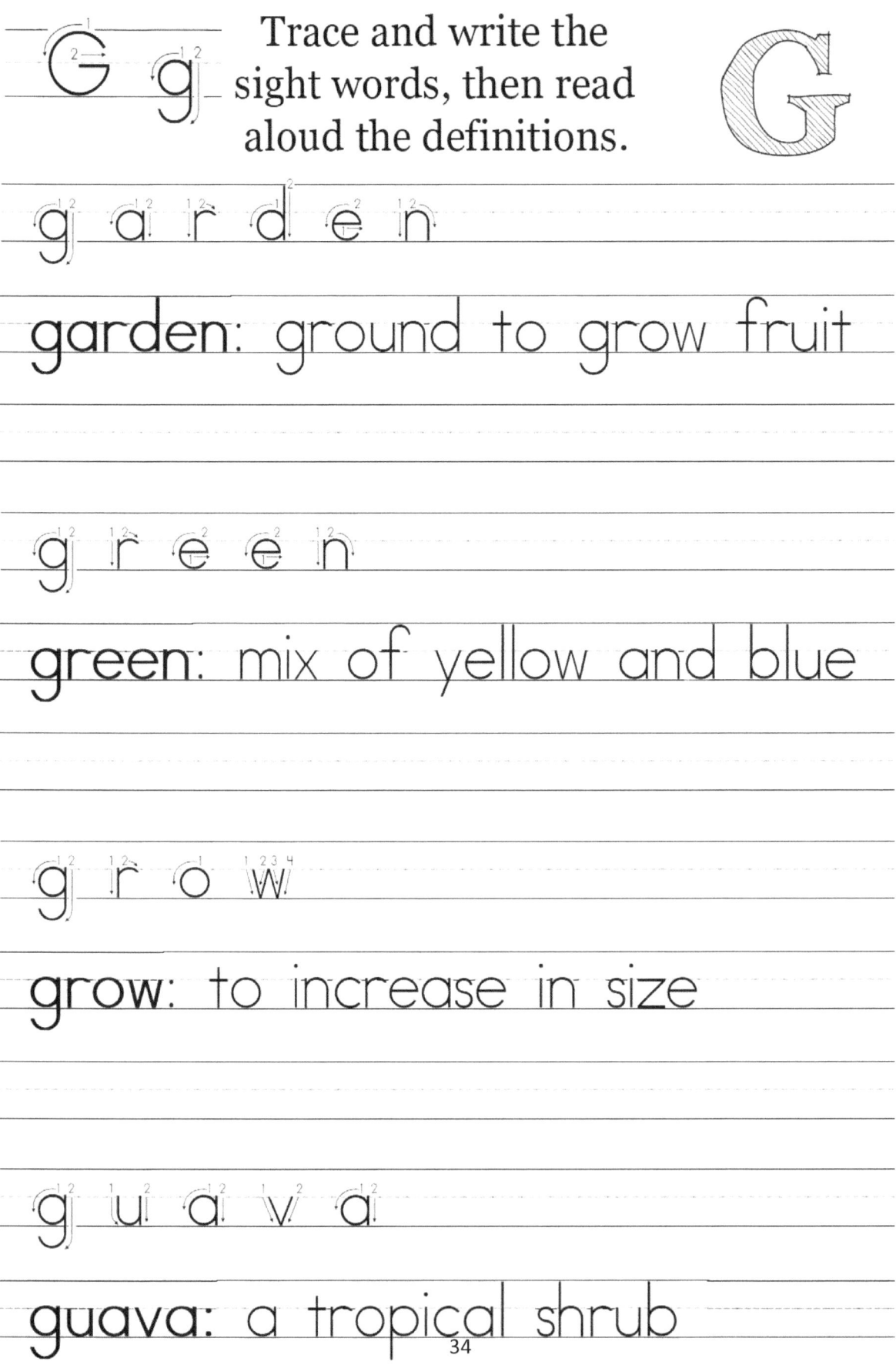

G g

G

garden

garden: ground to grow fruit

green

green: mix of yellow and blue

grow

grow: to increase in size

guava

guava: a tropical shrub

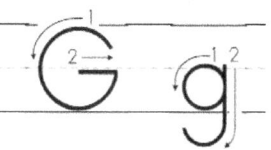 

Use the examples below to help write new sentences.

The boy walked in a garden.

The piece of guava is green.

I grow fruit in my garden.

H h

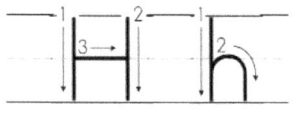

Practice tracing the letters and then write them.

H H H H H H

H

H H H H H H

H

h h h h h h

h

h h h h h h

h

horned melon

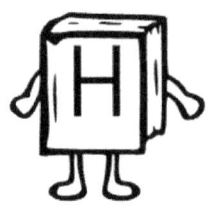

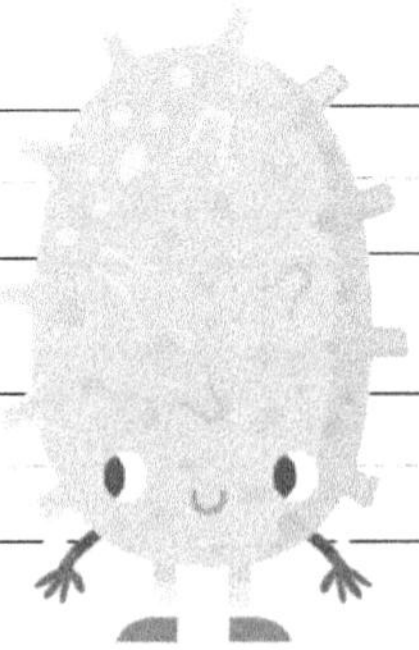

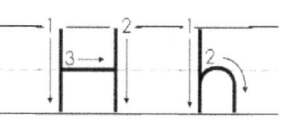

Practice tracing the sight words and then write them.

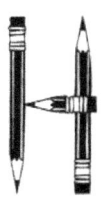

had

had

half

half

his

his

horned melon

horned melon

Trace and write the sight words, then read aloud the definitions.

had

had: past tense of have

half

half: one of two equal parts

his

his: belonging to him

horned melon

horned melon: spiked fruit

38

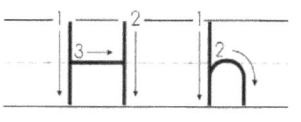 **Use the examples below to help write new sentences.**

She had one horned melon.

I ate half of a horned melon.

He ate half of his lunch.

BONUS WORDS FROM THE DANGER TWINS

The Danger Twins listed bonus sight words below. Write a sentence using any of the sight words.

girl   home

good   happy

gave   hat

Practice tracing the letters and then write them.

i m b e

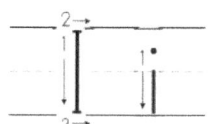

idea

idea

in

in

it

it

imbe

imbe

I i

Trace and write the
sight words, then read
aloud the definitions.

I

idea

idea: a thought

in

in: on the inside

it

it: an inanimate thing

imbe

imbe: a fruit tree

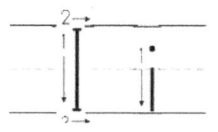

Use the examples
below to help write
new sentences.

The girl has a good idea.

He has an **imbe in** his lunch.

I will fix **it** today.

J j

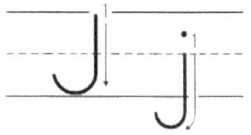

Practice tracing the letters and then write them.

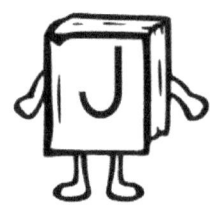

J J J J J J

J

J J J J J J

J

j j j j j j

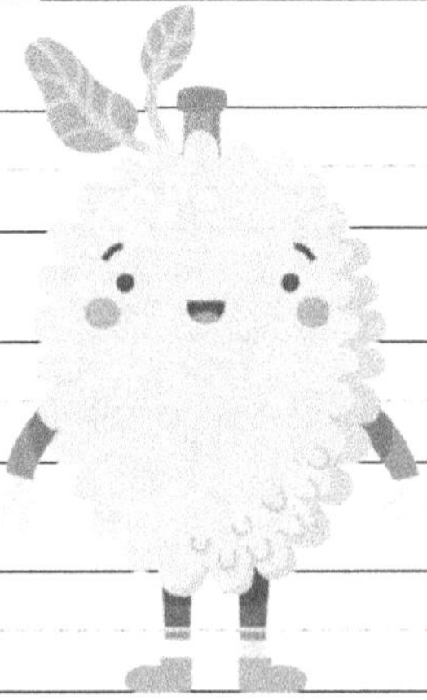

j

j j j j j j

j

j a c k f r u i t

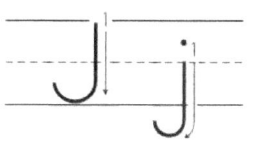

Practice tracing the sight words and then write them.

join

join

juice

juice

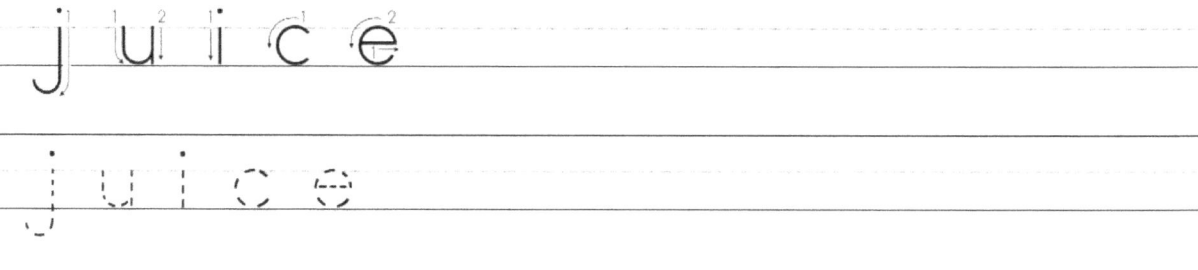

just

just

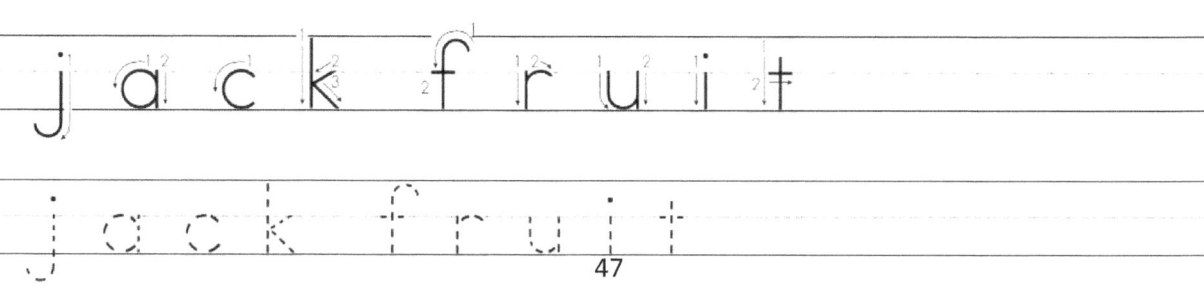

jack fruit

jack fruit

 Trace and write the
sight words, then read
aloud the definitions.
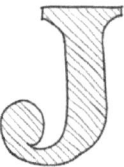

join

join: to bring into contact

juice

juice: liquid from fruit

just

just: guided by truth

jack fruit

jack fruit: a type of fig tree

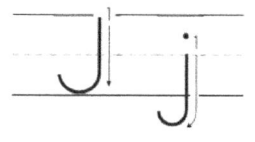

Use the examples
below to help write
new sentences.

Please join the group.

He just wants some juice.

We like to eat jack fruit.

BONUS WORDS FROM THE DANGER TWINS

The Danger Twins listed bonus sight words below. Write a sentence using any of the sight words.

into   jog

ice   jump

inside   jam

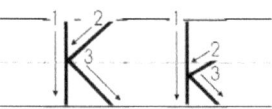

Practice tracing the letters and then write them.

K K K K K K K

K

K K K K K

k k k k k k

k

k k k k k

k i w i

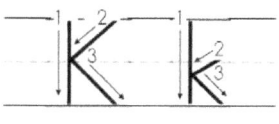 **Practice tracing the sight words and then write them.**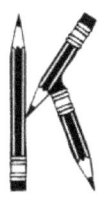

keep

keep

kind

kind

knew

knew

kiwi

kiwi

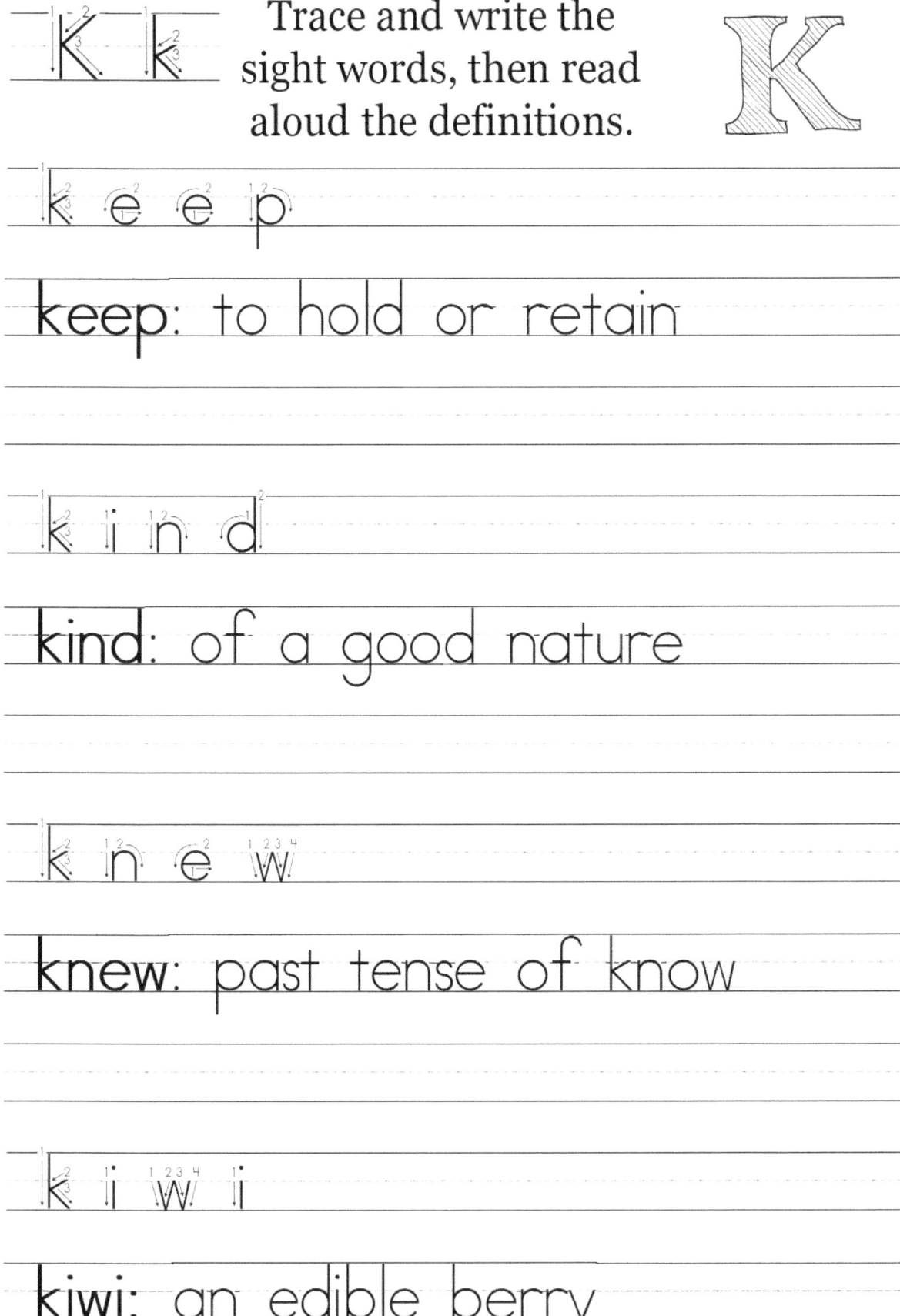

K k

Trace and write the sight words, then read aloud the definitions.

keep

keep: to hold or retain

kind

kind: of a good nature

knew

knew: past tense of know

kiwi

kiwi: an edible berry

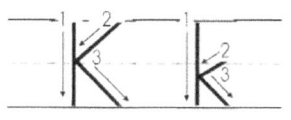 Use the examples
below to help write
new sentences.

Please **keep** your room clean.

She was **kind** to everyone.

I **knew** that was a **kiwi**.

L l

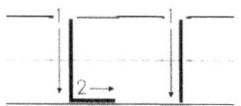

Practice tracing the letters and then write them.

L L L L L L

L L L L L L

l l l l l l

l l l l l l

l e m o n

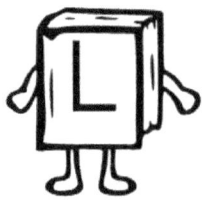

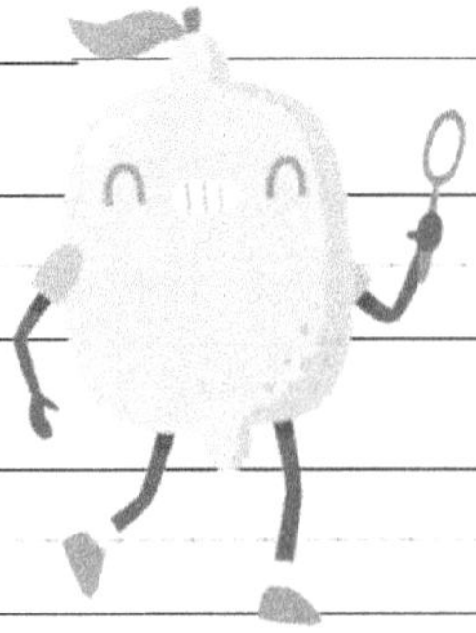

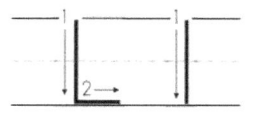

Practice tracing the sight words and then write them.

lady

lady

little

little

love

love

lemon

lemon

L l

Trace and write the sight words, then read aloud the definitions.

l a d y

lady: a refined woman

l i t t l e

little: small in size

l o v e

love: deep feeling for another

l e m o n

lemon: yellow citrus fruit

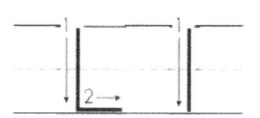

Use the examples below to help write new sentences.

A lady cut the lemon.

The lemon is a little fruit.

I love my entire family.

BONUS WORDS FROM THE DANGER TWINS

The Danger Twins listed bonus sight words below. Write a sentence using any of the sight words.

key   like

kept   less

know   last

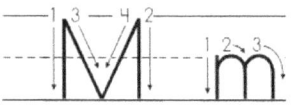 

Practice tracing the letters and then write them.

M M M M M M

M

M M M M M M

M

m m m m m m

m

m m m m m m

m

mango

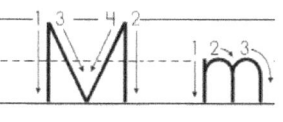 Practice tracing
the sight words and
then write them.
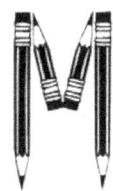

men

men

milk

milk

more

more

mango

mango

63

M m

Trace and write the sight words, then read aloud the definitions.

m e n

men: plural of man

m i l k

milk: white liquid

m o r e

more: in greater quantity

m a n g o

mango: sweet tropical fruit

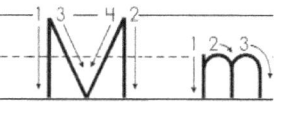 

Use the examples below to help write new sentences.

The men cut open a mango.

She drank a glass of milk.

I wish we had more mango.

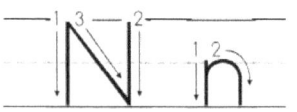

Practice tracing the letters and then write them.

N N N N N N N

N

N N N N N N N

N

n n n n n n

n

n n n n n n

n

n u n g u

66

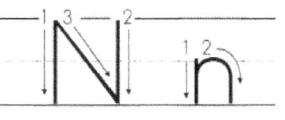 **Practice tracing the sight words and then write them.**

need

need

never

never

new

new

nungu

nungu

Nn

Trace and write the sight words, then read aloud the definitions.

n e e d

need: something you require

n e v e r

never: at no time

n e w

new: opposite of old

n u n g u

nungu: an ice apple

Use the examples below to help write new sentences.

We need to try new fruits.

I have never tried nungu.

She likes the new foods.

The Danger Twins listed bonus sight words below. Write a sentence using any of the sight words.

mine   not

me   natural

made   nose

Practice tracing the letters and then write them.

o r a n g e

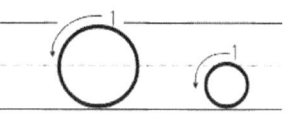 # Practice tracing the sight words and then write them.

on

on

one

one

outside

outside

orange

orange

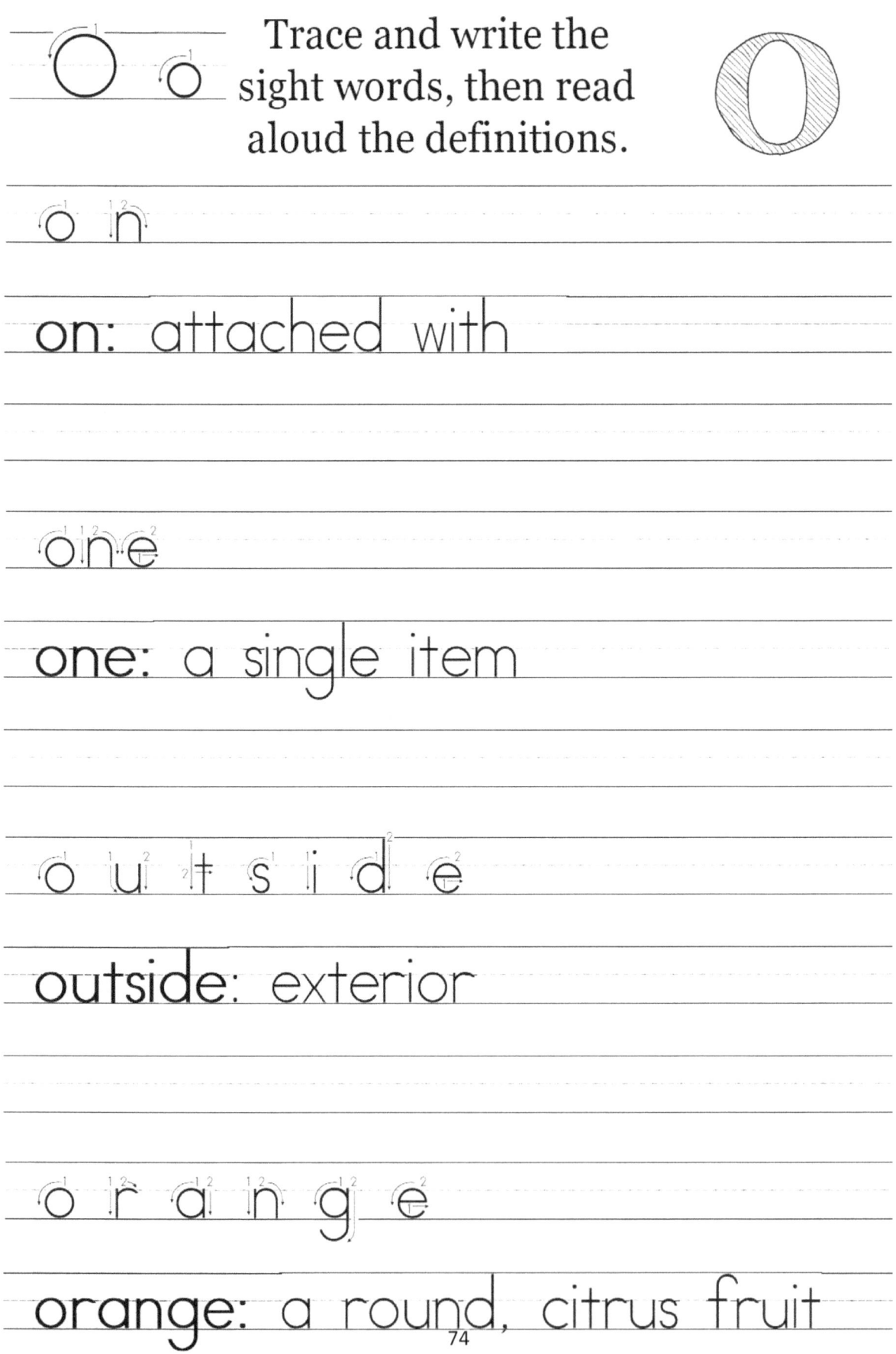

Trace and write the
sight words, then read
aloud the definitions.

o n

on: attached with

one

one: a single item

outside

outside: exterior

orange

orange: a round, citrus fruit

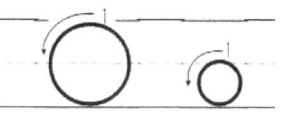

Use the examples
below to help write
new sentences.

The girl ate **on** the table.

He ate **one orange**.

She walked **outside**.

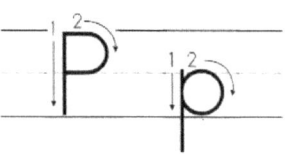

Practice tracing the letters and then write them.

P P P P P P P

P

P P P P P P

P

p p p p p p

p

p p p p p p

p

pineapple

76

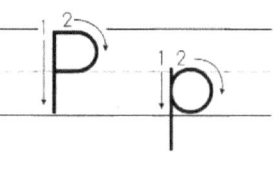

Practice tracing the sight words and then write them.

picked

picked

piece

piece

play

play

pineapple

pineapple

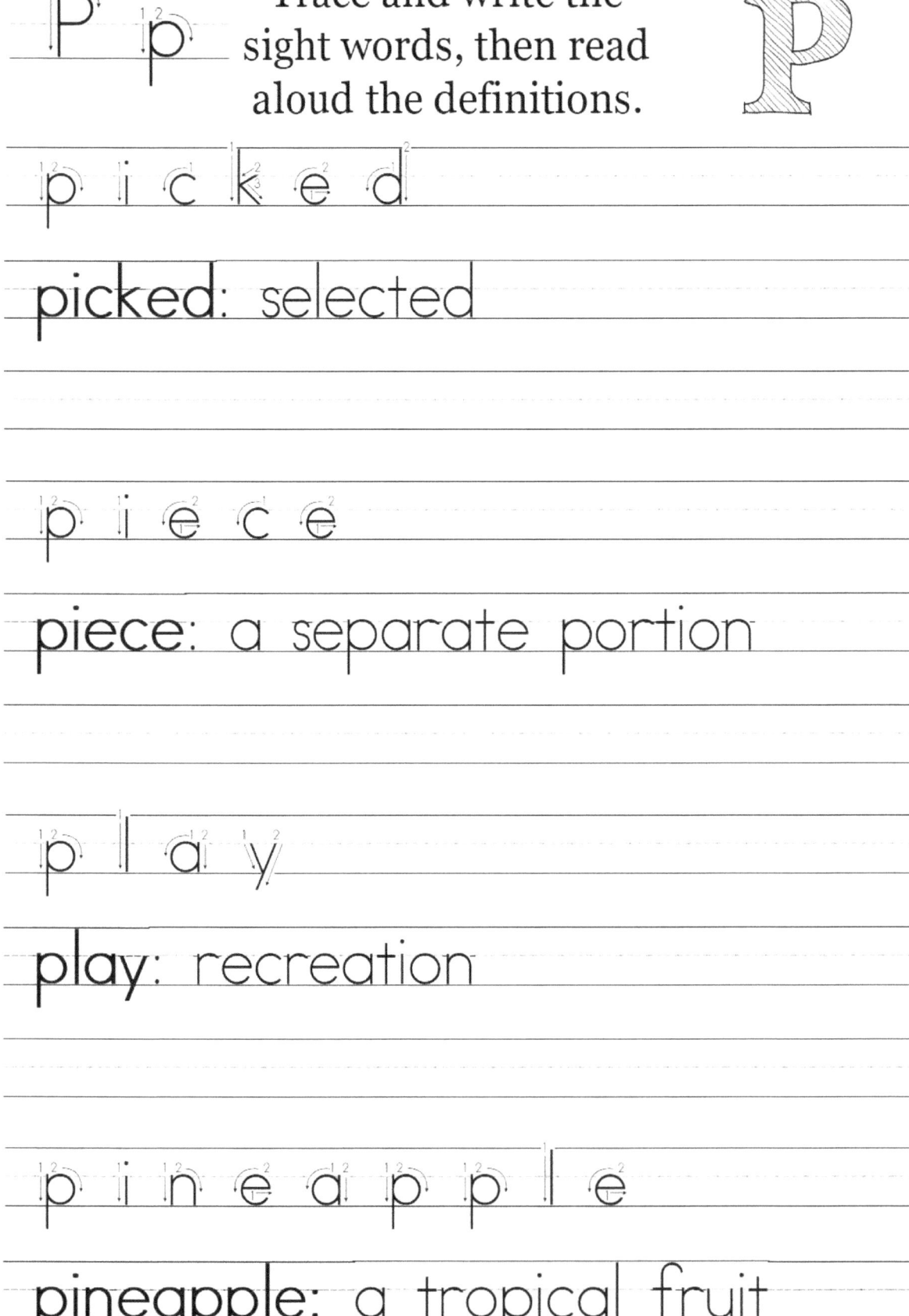

Pp Trace and write the sight words, then read aloud the definitions. P

picked

picked: selected

piece

piece: a separate portion

play

play: recreation

pineapple

pineapple: a tropical fruit

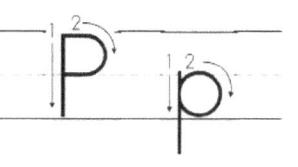 

Use the examples below to help write new sentences.

He picked up the pineapple.

I ate a piece of pineapple.

She likes to play in my yard.

BONUS WORDS FROM THE DANGER TWINS

The Danger Twins listed bonus sight words below. Write a sentence using any of the sight words.

one   part

off   place

order   pay

Q q

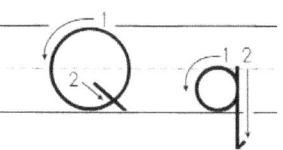

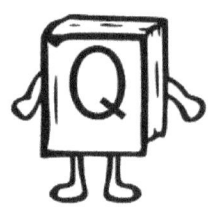

Practice tracing the letters and then write them.

Q Q Q Q Q Q

Q

Q Q Q Q Q Q

Q

q q q q q q

q

q q q q q q

q

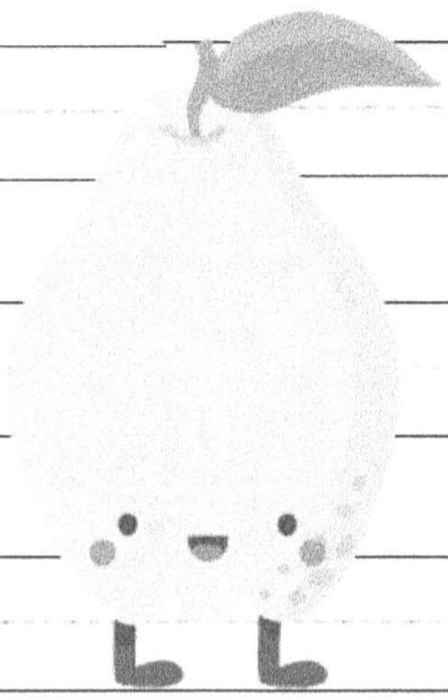

quince

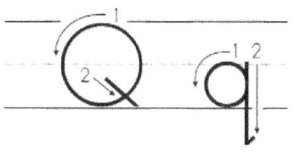

Practice tracing the sight words and then write them.

question

question

quick

quick

quiet

quiet

quince

quince

Q q

Trace and write the sight words, then read aloud the definitions.

Q

question

question: ask for something

quick

quick: very fast

quiet

quiet: without sound

quince

quince: a round, edible fruit

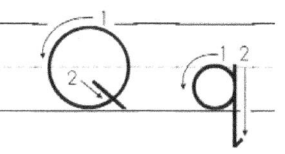

Use the examples below to help write new sentences.

Each girl asked a **question**.

He was both **quiet** and **quick**.

The boy ate his **quince**.

 **Practice tracing
the letters and
then write them.**

R R R R R R

R

R R R R R R

R

r r r r r r

r

r r r r r r

r

r a m b u t a n

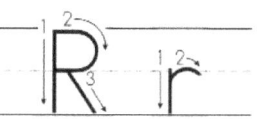 **Practice tracing the sight words and then write them.**

red

red

round

round

run

run

rambutan

rambutan

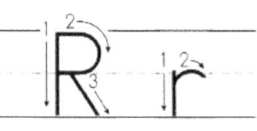 Trace and write the
sight words, then read
aloud the definitions.

r e d

red: color of a firetruck

r o u n d

round: circle, ring, or sphere

r u n

run: move your legs quickly

r a m b u t a n

rambutan: a red oval fruit

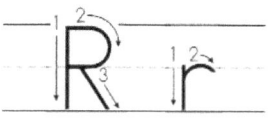 Use the examples
below to help write
new sentences.

A rambutan is **red** and tasty.

The **red** balloon is **round**.

I like to **run** in the yard.

BONUS WORDS FROM THE DANGER TWINS

The Danger Twins listed bonus sight words below. Write a sentence using any of the sight words.

quite   root

quest   rose

quell   rain

S s

Practice tracing the letters and then write them.

S S S S S S

S

S S S S S S

S

S S S S S S

S

S S S S S S

S

s t a r f r u i t

S s

Practice tracing the sight words and then write them.

s h e

s h e

s m a l l

s m a l l

s u n

s u n

s t a r f r u i t

s t a r f r u i t

S s S s

Trace and write the sight words, then read aloud the definitions.

S

s h e

she: a female person

s m a l l

small: of limited size

s u n

sun: main body in solar system

s t a r   f r u i t

star fruit: pointy, edible fruit

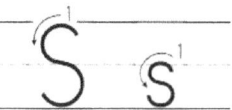

Use the examples
below to help write
new sentences.

She ate the star fruit.

The star fruit is small.

The sun is very bright.

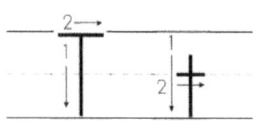

Practice tracing the letters and then write them.

T T T T T T

T

T T T T T T

T

t t t t t t

t

t t t t t t

t

tangerine

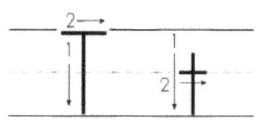 Practice tracing
the sight words and
then write them.

thin

thin

took

took

tree

tree

tangerine

tangerine

Trace and write the sight words, then read aloud the definitions.

T t

t h i n

thin: not thick

t o o k

took: past tense of take

t r e e

tree: a plant with a trunk

t a n g e r i n e

tangerine: a small orange

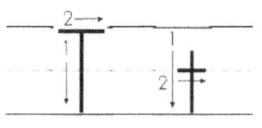 

Use the examples
below to help write
new sentences.

The tangerine peel is thin.

He took one tangerine.

Our tree branch is thin.

BONUS WORDS FROM THE DANGER TWINS

The Danger Twins listed bonus sight words below. Write a sentence using any of the sight words.

seeds   take

soft   table

show   turn

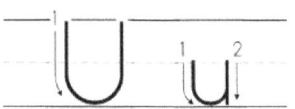

Practice tracing
the letters and
then write them.

U U U U U U

U

U U U U U U

U

u u u u u u

u

u u u u u u

u

u s u m a

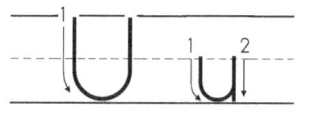

Practice tracing the sight words and then write them.

u p

u p

u s e

u s e

u n t i l

u n t i l

u s u m a

u s u m a

U u

Trace and write the sight words, then read aloud the definitions.

U

u p

up: to a higher position

u s e

use: to be of service

u n t i l

until: up to the time

u s u m a

usuma: an evergreen shrub

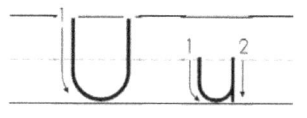 **Use the examples below to help write new sentences.**

A ripe **usuma** is **up** top.

We will **use** our forks.

I will not eat **until** dinner.

Practice tracing the letters and then write them.

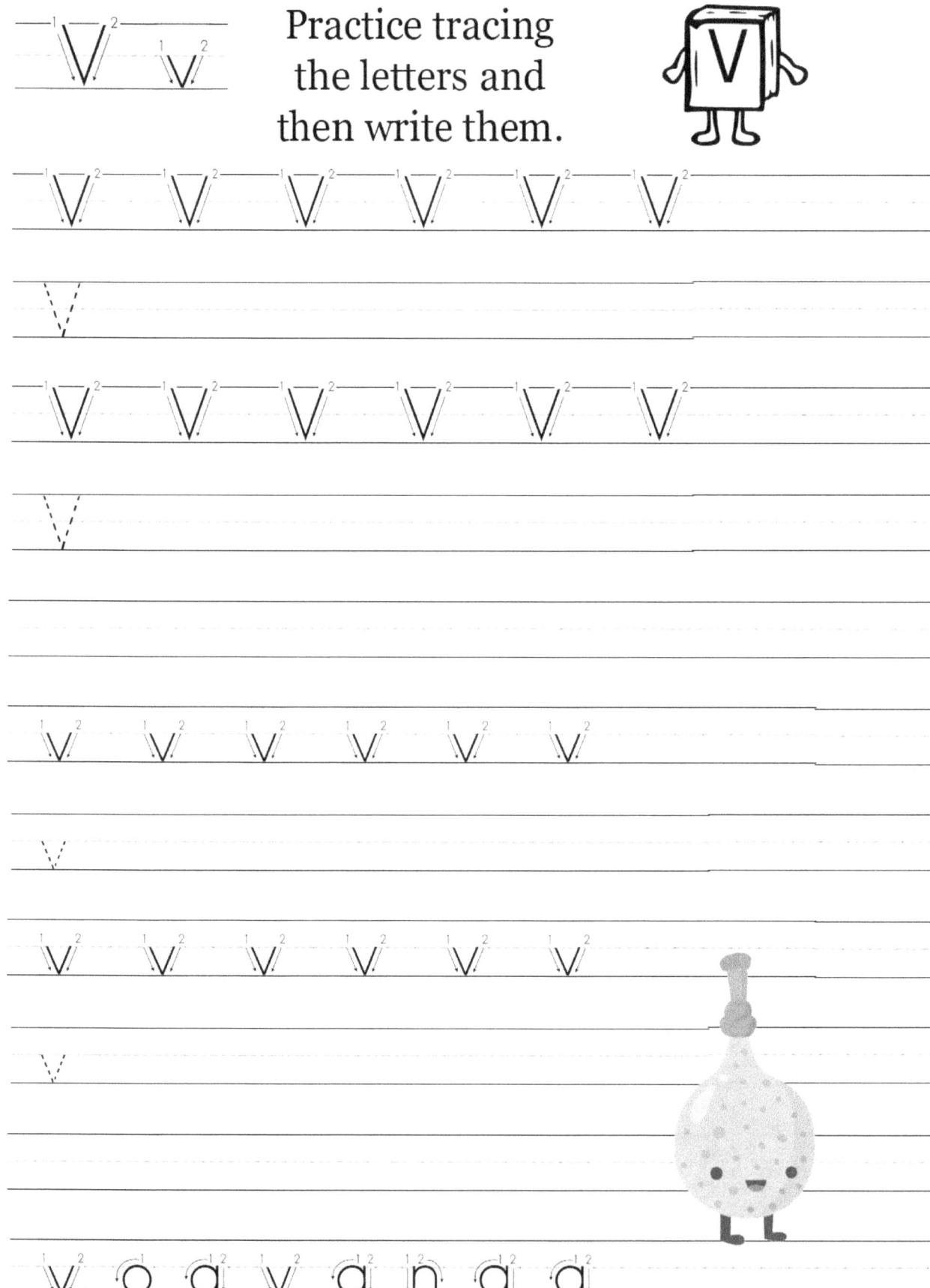

V V V V V V V

V

V V V V V

V

v v v v v v

v

v v v v v v

v

voavanga

106

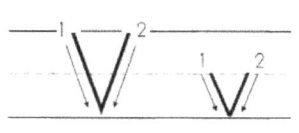

Practice tracing the sight words and then write them.

very

very

vine

vine

visit

visit

voavanga

voavanga

V v Trace and write the sight words, then read aloud the definitions.

v e r y

very: precise

v i n e

vine: a long stem

v i s i t

visit: to stay as a guest

v o a v a n g a

vaovanga: similar to grapefruit

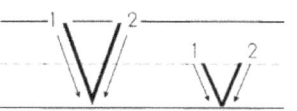

Use the examples
below to help write
new sentences.

A voavanga is very good.

The vine is very long.

Our visit was very nice.

BONUS WORDS FROM THE DANGER TWINS

The Danger Twins listed bonus sight words below. Write a sentence using any of the sight words.

under   view

upon   voice

us   various

W w

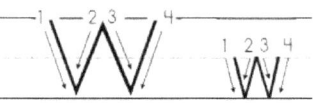

Practice tracing the letters and then write them.

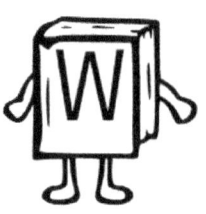

W W W W W

W

W W W W W

W

w w w w w w

w

w w w w w w

w

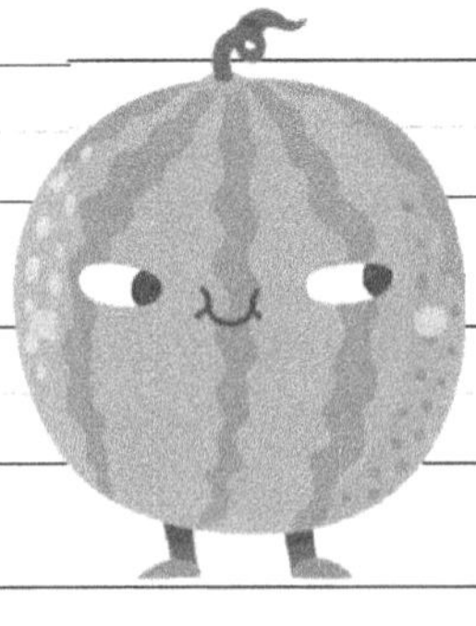

w a t e r m e l o n

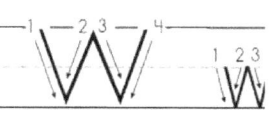
Practice tracing the sight words and then write them.

water

water

wide

wide

work

work

watermelon

watermelon

Ww

Trace and write the sight words, then read aloud the definitions.

water

water: clear liquid

wide

wide: great distance

work

work: put forth effort

watermelon

watermelon: a large gourd

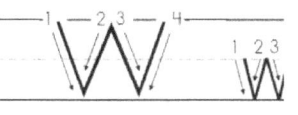 

Use the examples below to help write new sentences.

The girl drank the **water**.

That **watermelon** is wide.

I have a lot of **work** to do.

X x

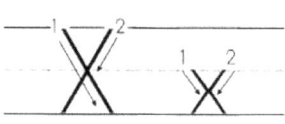

Practice tracing the letters and then write them.

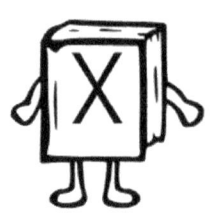

X X X X X X

X

X X X X X X

X

x x x x x x

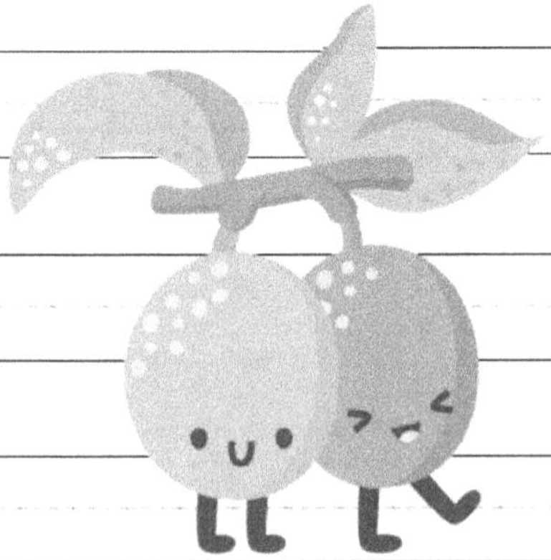

x

x x x x x x

x

x i m e n i a

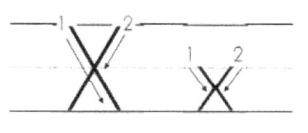 **Practice tracing the sight words and then write them.**

x e n o p s

x e n o p s

x-r a y

x-r a y

x y r i s

x y r i s

x i m e n i a

x i m e n i a

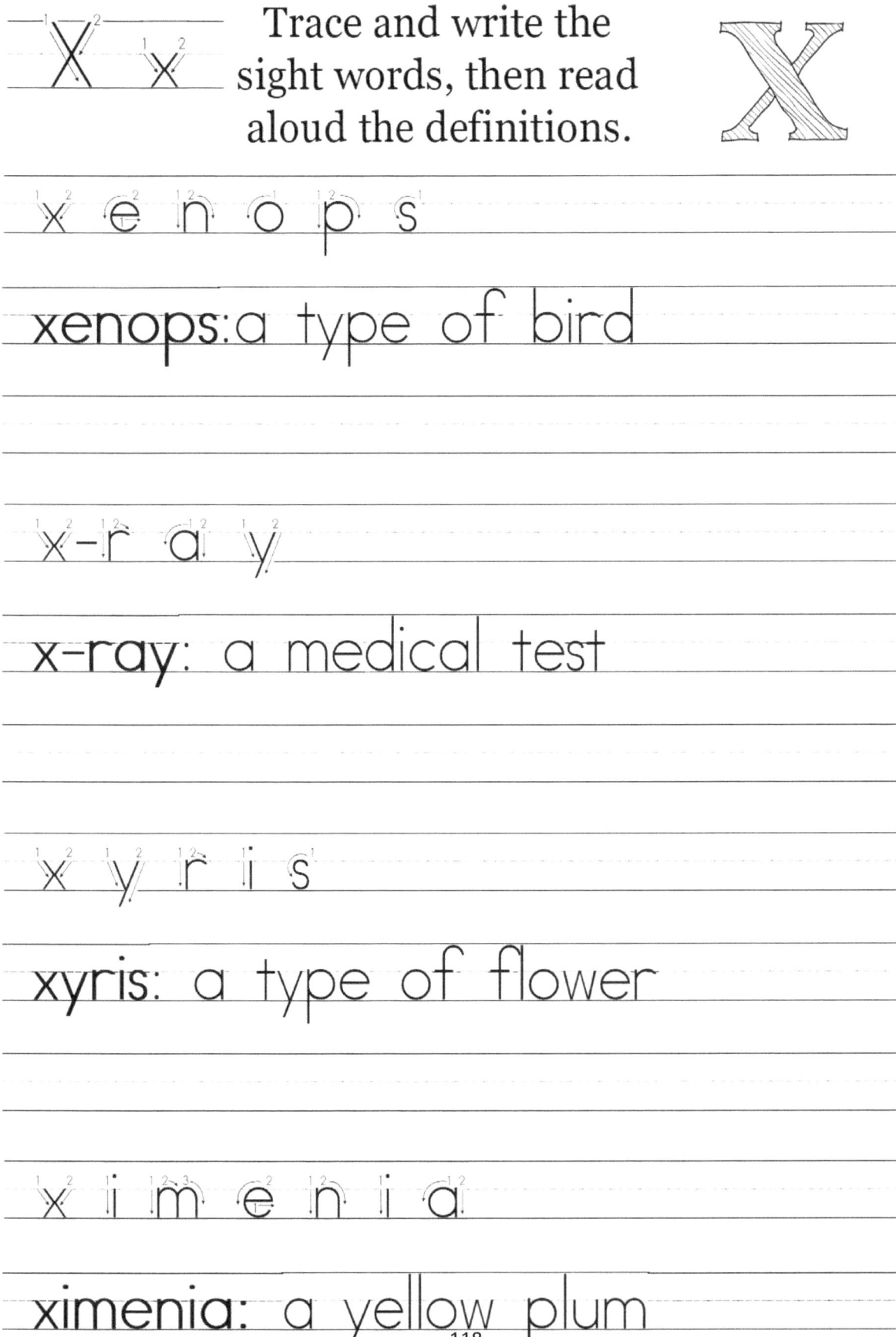

Trace and write the sight words, then read aloud the definitions.

X x

X

x e n o p s

xenops: a type of bird

x-r a y

x-ray: a medical test

x y r i s

xyris: a type of flower

x i m e n i a

ximenia: a yellow plum

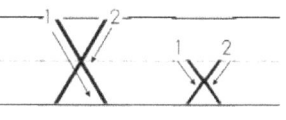 Use the examples
below to help write
new sentences.

I saw an **xenops** and xyris.

He had an x-ray taken.

She ate the ximenia.

BONUS WORDS FROM THE DANGER TWINS

The Danger Twins listed bonus sight words below. Write a sentence using any of the sight words.

we   boxes

want   exit

wait   next

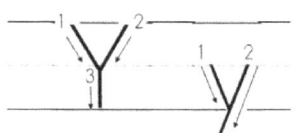

Practice tracing the letters and then write them.

Y Y Y Y Y Y

Y

Y Y Y Y Y Y

Y

y y y y y y

y

y y y y y y

y

y u z u

122

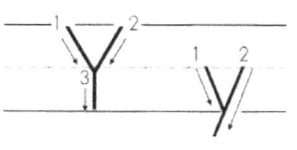 **Practice tracing the sight words and then write them.**

yard

yard

yellow

yellow

your

your

yuzu

yuzu

Trace and write the sight words, then read aloud the definitions.

Y y   Y

y a r d

yard: land around your home

y e l l o w

yellow: color of a banana

y o u r

your: belong to any person

y u z u

yuzu: a citrus fruit

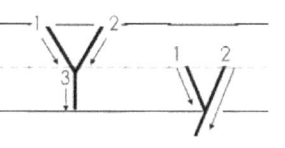 Use the examples
below to help write
new sentences.

Your house has a big **yard.**

The fresh **yuzu** tastes good.

We ate a **yellow** banana.

Zz

Practice tracing the letters and then write them.

Z Z Z Z Z Z Z

Z

Z Z Z Z Z Z Z

Z

z z z z z z

z

z z z z z z

z

z i z i p h u s

126

Zz

Practice tracing the sight words and then write them.

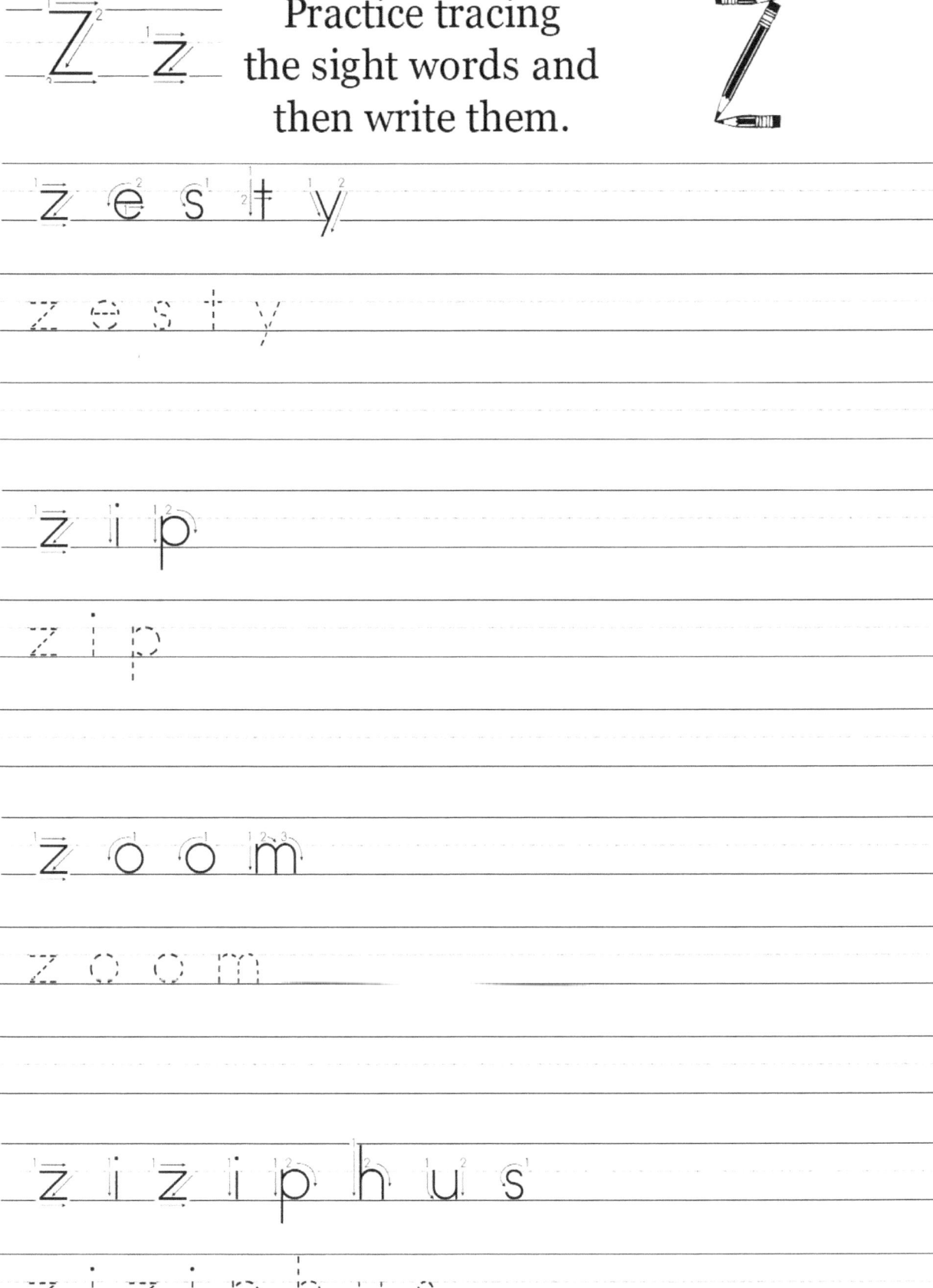

zesty

zesty

zip

zip

zoom

zoom

ziziphus

ziziphus

Zz Trace and write the sight words, then read aloud the definitions.

Z

zesty

zesty: energetic

zip

zip: to move with energy

zoom

zoom: to move quickly

ziziphus

ziziphus: a round, red fruit

Z z Use the examples
below to help write
new sentences.

The girls were zesty.

The boy could zip and zoom.

The ziziphus was tasty.

BONUS WORDS FROM THE DANGER TWINS

The Danger Twins listed bonus sight words below. Write a sentence using any of the sight words.

yes   zap

you   zany

years   zoo

theDangerTwins.com

www.ingramcontent.com/pod-product-compliance
Lightning Source LLC
Chambersburg PA
CBHW080959120626
46546CB00010B/2964